P9-DMB-942

Santa's Favorite Cookies

Sweet Treats for the Christmas Season

PUBLICATIONS INTERNATIONAL, LTD.

Copyright © 1999 Publications International, Ltd.
All rights reserved. This publication may not be reproduced or quoted in whole or in part by any means whatsoever without written permission from:

Louis Weber, CEO
Publications International, Ltd.
7373 North Cicero Avenue
Lincolnwood, Illinois 60712

Permission is never granted for commercial purposes.

All recipes and photographs that contain specific brand names are copyrighted by those companies and/or associations, unless otherwise specified. All photographs *except* those on pages 9, 21 and 45 copyright © Publications International, Ltd.

DOLE® is a registered trademark of Dole Food Company, Inc.

Some of the products listed in this publication may be in limited distribution.

Front cover photography by Peter Walters Photography/Chicago.

Pictured on the front cover *(clockwise from top):* Decadent Brownies *(page 10),* Jolly Peanut Butter Gingerbread Cookies *(page 68),* Almond Milk Chocolate Chippers *(page 30),* Yuletide Linzer Bars *(page 16),* Mocha Crinkles *(page 28),* Peanut Butter Chocolate Chippers *(page 24)* and Candy Cane Cookies *(page 54).*

Pictured on the back cover *(clockwise from top left):* Christmas Tree Platter *(page 76),* Slice 'n' Bake Ginger Wafers *(page 58)* and Festive Fudge Blossoms *(page 40).*

ISBN: 0-7853-3816-0

Manufactured in China.

8 7 6 5 4 3 2 1

Microwave Cooking: Microwave ovens vary in wattage. Use the cooking times as guidelines and check for doneness before adding more time.

Santa's Favorite Cookies

Sweet Treats for the Christmas Season

Brownies & Bars

Mystical Layered Bars

⅓ cup margarine or butter
1 cup graham cracker crumbs
½ cup old-fashioned or quick oats
1 can (14 ounces) sweetened condensed milk
1 cup flaked coconut
¾ cup semisweet chocolate chips
¾ cup raisins
1 cup coarsely chopped pecans

Preheat oven to 350°F. Melt margarine in 13×9-inch baking pan. Remove from oven. Sprinkle graham cracker crumbs and oats evenly over margarine; press down with fork. Drizzle condensed milk over oats. Layer coconut, chocolate chips, raisins and pecans over milk. Bake 25 to 30 minutes or until lightly browned. Cool in pan on wire rack 5 minutes. Cut into bars; cool completely.

Makes 3 dozen bars

Praline Brownies

Brownies

1 package DUNCAN HINES®
   Chocolate Lovers' Milk
   Chocolate Chunk Brownie Mix
2 eggs
⅓ cup water
⅓ cup canola oil plus additional for
   greasing
¾ cup chopped pecans

Topping

¾ cup firmly packed brown sugar
¾ cup chopped pecans
¼ cup butter or margarine, melted
2 tablespoons milk
½ teaspoon vanilla extract

1. Preheat oven to 350°F. Grease 9-inch square pan.

2. For brownies, combine brownie mix, eggs, water, oil and ¾ cup pecans in large bowl. Stir with spoon until well blended, about 50 strokes. Spread in prepared pan. Bake at 350°F for 35 to 40 minutes. Remove from oven.

3. For topping, combine brown sugar, ¾ cup pecans, melted butter, milk and vanilla extract in medium bowl. Stir with spoon until well blended. Spread over hot brownies. Return to oven. Bake for 15 minutes longer or until topping is set. Cool completely in pan on wire rack. Cut into bars.   *Makes about 16 brownies*

Chocolate Peanut Bars

½ cup butter or margarine, softened
¼ cup granulated sugar
1 cup packed brown sugar, divided
2 eggs, separated
1 teaspoon vanilla
2 cups all-purpose flour
2 teaspoons baking powder
½ teaspoon baking soda
¼ teaspoon salt
2 to 4 tablespoons milk
1 cup (6 ounces) semisweet
   chocolate chips
¾ cup salted peanuts, coarsely
   chopped

Preheat oven to 350°F. Lightly grease a 13×9-inch pan. Beat butter, granulated sugar and ¼ cup of brown sugar in large bowl. Beat in egg yolks and vanilla. Combine flour, baking powder, baking soda and salt in small bowl. Blend into butter mixture. Stir in enough milk to make a smooth, light dough. Press on bottom of prepared pan. Sprinkle chocolate chips over top; press lightly into dough. Beat egg whites in large bowl until stiff, but not dry. Gradually beat in remaining ¾ cup brown sugar. Spread mixture evenly over dough in pan; top with peanuts. Bake 25 to 30 minutes or until top is puffed, lightly browned and feels dry. Cut into 2×1-inch bars while still warm.
      Makes about 5 dozen bars

Praline Brownies

Luscious Lemon Bars

Grated peel from 2 lemons
2 cups all-purpose flour
1 cup butter
½ cup powdered sugar
¼ teaspoon salt
1 cup granulated sugar
3 eggs
⅓ cup fresh lemon juice
Powdered sugar

1. Preheat oven to 350°F. Grease 13×9-inch baking pan; set aside. Place 1 teaspoon lemon peel, flour, butter, powdered sugar and salt in food processor. Process until mixture forms coarse crumbs.

2. Press mixture evenly into prepared 13×9-inch baking pan. Bake 18 to 20 minutes or until golden brown.

3. Beat 3 teaspoons lemon peel, granulated sugar, eggs and lemon juice in medium bowl with electric mixer at medium speed until well blended.

4. Pour mixture evenly over warm crust. Return to oven; bake 18 to 20 minutes or until center is set and edges are golden brown. Remove pan to wire rack; cool completely.

5. Dust with powdered sugar; cut into 2×1½-inch bars. Do not freeze.

Makes 3 dozen bars

Decadent Brownies

½ cup dark corn syrup
½ cup butter or margarine
6 squares (1 ounce *each*) semisweet chocolate
¾ cup sugar
3 eggs
1 cup all-purpose flour
1 cup chopped walnuts
1 teaspoon vanilla
Fudge Glaze (recipe follows)

Preheat oven to 350°F. Grease 8-inch square pan. Combine corn syrup, butter and chocolate in large heavy saucepan. Place over low heat; stir until chocolate is melted and ingredients are blended. Remove from heat; blend in sugar. Stir in eggs, flour, chopped walnuts and vanilla. Spread batter evenly in prepared pan. Bake 20 to 25 minutes or just until center is set. *Do not overbake.* Meanwhile, prepare Fudge Glaze. Remove brownies from oven. Immediately spread glaze evenly over hot brownies. Cool in pan on wire rack. Cut into 2-inch squares.

Makes 16 brownies

Fudge Glaze

3 squares (1 ounce *each*) semisweet chocolate
2 tablespoons dark corn syrup
1 tablespoon butter or margarine
1 teaspoon light cream or milk

Combine chocolate, corn syrup and butter in small heavy saucepan. Stir over low heat until smooth; add cream.

Luscious Lemon Bars

Caramel Fudge Brownies

1 jar (12 ounces) hot caramel ice
    cream topping
1¼ cups all-purpose flour, divided
¼ teaspoon baking powder
    Dash salt
4 squares (1 ounce *each*)
    unsweetened chocolate,
    coarsely chopped
¾ cup butter or margarine
2 cups sugar
3 eggs
2 teaspoons vanilla
¾ cup semisweet chocolate chips
¾ cup chopped pecans

Preheat oven to 350°F. Lightly grease
13×9-inch baking pan.

Combine caramel topping and ¼ cup
flour in small bowl; set aside.

Combine remaining 1 cup flour, baking
powder and salt in small bowl; mix well.

Place unsweetened chocolate squares
and margarine in medium microwavable
bowl. Microwave at HIGH 2 minutes or
until margarine is melted; stir until
chocolate is completely melted.

Stir sugar into melted chocolate with
mixing spoon. Add eggs and vanilla; stir
until combined.

Add flour mixture, stirring until well
blended. Spread chocolate mixture
evenly into prepared pan.

Bake 25 minutes. Immediately after
removing brownies from oven, spread
caramel mixture over brownies. Sprinkle
top evenly with chocolate chips and
pecans.

Return pan to oven; bake 20 to
25 minutes or until topping is golden
brown and bubbling. *Do not overbake.*
Cool brownies completely in pan on wire
rack. Cut into 2×1½-inch bars.
Makes 3 dozen brownies

Almond Toffee Bars

¾ cup butter or margarine, softened
¾ cup packed brown sugar
1½ cups all-purpose flour
½ teaspoon almond extract
½ teaspoon vanilla extract
¼ teaspoon salt
1 package (6 ounces) semi-sweet
    real chocolate pieces
¾ cup BLUE DIAMOND® Chopped
    Natural Almonds, toasted

Preheat oven to 350°F. Cream butter and
sugar; blend in flour. Add extracts and
salt, mixing well. Spread in bottom of
ungreased 13×9×2-inch baking pan.
Bake in 350°F oven 15 to 20 minutes or
until deep golden brown. Remove from
oven and sprinkle with chocolate pieces.
When chocolate has melted, spread
evenly; sprinkle with almonds. Cut into
bars; cool.   *Makes about 40 bars*

Caramel Fudge Brownies

Raspberry & White Chip Nut Bars

1⅔ cups (10-ounce package) HERSHEY'S Premier White Chips, divided
¾ cup (1½ sticks) butter or margarine
2¼ cups all-purpose flour
¾ cup sugar
3 eggs
¾ teaspoon baking powder
1⅔ cups (10-ounce package) HERSHEY'S Raspberry Chips, divided
½ cup chopped pecans
Double Drizzle (recipe follows)

1. Heat oven to 350°F. Grease 13×9×2-inch baking pan.

2. Reserve 2 tablespoons white chips for drizzle. Place remaining white chips and butter in medium microwave-safe bowl. Microwave at HIGH (100%) 1½ minutes; stir. If necessary, microwave at HIGH an additional 15 seconds at a time, stirring after each heating, just until chips are melted when stirred. Combine flour, sugar, eggs and baking powder in large bowl. Add white chip mixture; beat well. Reserve 2 tablespoons raspberry chips for drizzle. Chop remaining raspberry chips in food processor; stir into batter with pecans. Spread into pan.

3. Bake 25 minutes or until edges pull away from sides of pan and top surface is golden. Cool completely in pan on wire rack. Prepare Double Drizzle; using one flavor at a time, drizzle over top of bars. Cut into bars.

Makes about 24 bars

Double Drizzle: Place 2 tablespoons HERSHEY'S Premier White Chips and ½ teaspoon shortening (do not use butter, margarine or oil) in small microwave-safe bowl. Microwave at HIGH (100%) 1 minute; stir. If necessary, microwave at HIGH an additional 15 seconds at a time, stirring after each heating, just until chips are melted when stirred. Repeat with raspberry chips.

Peanut Butter and Chocolate Bars: Omit HERSHEY'S Premier White Chips; replace with REESE'S® Peanut Butter Chips. Omit HERSHEY'S Raspberry Chips; replace with HERSHEY'S Semi-Sweet Chocolate Chips. Omit chopped pecans; replace with ½ cup chopped peanuts.

Butterscotch and Chocolate Bars: Omit HERSHEY'S Premier White Chips; replace with HERSHEY'S Butterscotch Chips. Omit HERSHEY'S Raspberry Chips; replace with HERSHEY'S Semi-Sweet Chocolate Chips. Omit chopped pecans; replace with ½ cup chopped walnuts.

Madison Avenue Mocha Brownies

1 (20- to 23-ounce) package
    brownie mix
1 (8-ounce) package
    PHILADELPHIA® Cream Cheese,
    softened
⅓ cup sugar
1 egg
1½ teaspoons MAXWELL HOUSE®
    Instant Coffee
1 teaspoon vanilla

Preheat oven to 350°F.

Prepare brownie mix according to package directions. Pour into greased 13×9-inch baking pan.

Beat cream cheese, sugar and egg in small mixing bowl at medium speed with electric mixer until well blended.

Dissolve coffee in vanilla; add to cream cheese mixture, mixing until well blended.

Spoon cream cheese mixture over brownie batter; cut through batter with knife several times for marble effect.

Bake 35 to 40 minutes or until set. Cool in pan on wire rack. Cut into bars.
Makes about 4 dozen brownies

Prep Time: 20 minutes
Cook Time: 40 minutes

Supreme Chocolate Saucepan Brownies

1 cup butter or margarine
2 cups sugar
½ cup HERSHEY'S Cocoa
4 eggs, beaten
⅔ cup all-purpose flour
½ teaspoon salt
¼ teaspoon baking soda
2 teaspoons vanilla extract
2 cups (12-ounce package)
    HERSHEY'S Semi-Sweet
    Chocolate Chips
½ cup macadamia nuts, coarsely
    chopped

1. Heat oven to 350°F. Grease 13×9×2-inch baking pan.

2. Melt butter in medium saucepan over low heat. Add sugar and cocoa; stir to blend. Remove from heat. Stir in eggs. Stir together flour, salt and baking soda; stir into chocolate mixture. Stir in vanilla, chocolate chips and nuts. Spread in prepared pan.

3. Bake 30 to 35 minutes or until brownies begin to pull away from sides of pan and begin to crack slightly; *do not underbake.* Cool completely; cut into bars.
Makes about 24 brownies

Yuletide Linzer Bars

1⅓ cups butter or margarine,
    softened
¾ cup sugar
1 egg
1 teaspoon grated lemon peel
2½ cups all-purpose flour
1½ cups whole almonds, ground
1 teaspoon ground cinnamon
¾ cup raspberry preserves
    Powdered sugar

Preheat oven to 350°F. Grease
13×9-inch baking pan.

Beat butter and sugar in large bowl with
electric mixer until creamy. Beat in egg
and lemon peel until blended. Mix in flour,
almonds and cinnamon until well blended.

Press 2 cups dough into bottom of
prepared pan. Spread preserves over
crust. Press remaining dough, a small
amount at a time, evenly over preserves.

Bake 35 to 40 minutes until golden
brown. Cool in pan on wire rack. Sprinkle
with powdered sugar; cut into bars.

Makes 36 bars

Black Russian Brownies

4 squares (1 ounce each)
    unsweetened chocolate
1 cup butter
¾ teaspoon ground black pepper
4 eggs, lightly beaten
1½ cups granulated sugar
1½ teaspoons vanilla
⅓ cup KAHLÚA® Liqueur
2 tablespoons vodka
1⅓ cups all-purpose flour
½ teaspoon salt
¼ teaspoon baking powder
1 cup chopped walnuts or toasted
    sliced almonds
    Powdered sugar (optional)

Preheat oven to 350°F. Line bottom of
13×9-inch baking pan with waxed paper.
Melt chocolate and butter with pepper in
small saucepan over low heat, stirring
until smooth. Remove from heat; cool.

Combine eggs, granulated sugar and
vanilla in large bowl; beat well. Stir in
cooled chocolate mixture, Kahlùa and
vodka. Combine flour, salt and baking
powder; add to chocolate mixture and
stir until blended. Add walnuts. Spread
evenly in prepared pan.

Bake just until wooden toothpick inserted
into center comes out clean, about
25 minutes. *Do not overbake.* Cool in pan
on wire rack. Cut into bars. Sprinkle with
powdered sugar.

Makes about 2½ dozen brownies

Yuletide Linzer Bars

Ooey Gooey Peanut Butter and Fudge Brownies

Batter

    WESSON® No-Stick Cooking
        Spray
    3 cups sugar
    1 cup (2 sticks) butter, softened
    ½ cup WESSON® Vegetable Oil
    1 tablespoon plus 1½ teaspoons
        vanilla
    6 eggs, at room temperature
    2¼ cups all-purpose flour
    1¼ cups cocoa
    1½ teaspoons baking powder
    ¾ teaspoon salt
    1 (10-ounce) bag peanut butter
        chips

Filling

    1½ cups PETER PAN® Creamy Peanut
        Butter
    ⅓ cup WESSON® Vegetable Oil
    ½ cup sugar
    3 tablespoons all-purpose flour
    3 eggs, at room temperature
    1 tablespoon vanilla

Frosting

    3 (1-ounce) bars unsweetened
        chocolate
    3 tablespoons PETER PAN® Creamy
        Peanut Butter
    2⅔ cups powdered sugar
    ¼ cup water
    1 teaspoon vanilla
    ¼ teaspoon salt

For batter, preheat oven to 350°F. Spray two 13×9×2-inch baking pans with Wesson® Cooking Spray. In a large bowl, beat sugar and butter until creamy. Add Wesson® Oil and vanilla. Add eggs, one at a time, beating well after each addition. In a small bowl, combine flour, cocoa, baking powder and salt; blend well. While beating, gradually add flour mixture to creamed mixture; mix well. Fold in peanut butter chips. Evenly spread ¼ of batter into one pan.

For filling, in a small bowl, cream together Peter Pan® Peanut Butter and Wesson® Oil. Add sugar and flour; blend well. Add eggs and vanilla; beat until smooth. Carefully spread ½ of filling mixture evenly over batter in pan. Top filling with an additional ¼ of batter and spread evenly. Gently cut through layers to create a marble effect throughout the brownies. Repeat process with remaining pan and remaining batter and remaining filling. Bake for 30 minutes. *Do not overbake.*

For frosting, meanwhile, in a medium saucepan, melt chocolate and peanut butter over LOW heat, stirring constantly. Remove from heat and stir in remaining ingredients; mix until smooth. If frosting is too thick, add an additional 1 to 3 tablespoons of water. Spread frosting over brownies immediately after baking. Cool in pans on wire racks.

Makes 3 dozen brownies

Ooey Gooey Peanut Butter and Fudge Brownies

Crimson Ribbon Bars

6 tablespoons butter or margarine, softened
½ cup firmly packed brown sugar
1 teaspoon vanilla
½ cup all-purpose flour
¼ teaspoon baking soda
1½ cups old-fashioned oats
1 cup chopped walnuts
**½ cup chopped BLUE RIBBON®
   Calimyrna or Mission Figs**
**⅓ cup SMUCKER'S® Red Raspberry
   Preserves**

Heat oven to 375°F. Combine butter, brown sugar and vanilla; beat until well blended. Add flour and baking soda; mix well. Stir in oats and walnuts. Reserve ¾ cup mixture for topping. Press remaining oat mixture into 8-inch square baking pan. Combine figs and preserves; spread mixture to within ½ inch of edges. Sprinkle with reserved oat mixture; press lightly. Bake 25 to 30 minutes or until golden brown. Cool in pan; cut into bars.

Makes 20 bars

Oreo® Shazam Bars

**28 OREO® Chocolate Sandwich
   Cookies**
¼ cup margarine, melted
1 cup shredded coconut
1 cup white chocolate chips
½ cup chopped nuts
**1 (14-ounce) can sweetened
   condensed milk**

Finely roll 20 cookies. Mix cookie crumbs and margarine; spread over bottom of 9×9×2-inch baking pan, pressing lightly. Chop remaining cookies. Layer coconut, chips, nuts and chopped cookies in prepared pan; drizzle evenly with condensed milk. Bake at 350°F for 25 to 30 minutes or until golden and set. Cool completely. Cut into bars.

Makes 24 bars

Cocoa Brownies

1¼ cups all-purpose flour
1 cup packed light brown sugar
¾ cup sugar
**½ cup EGG BEATERS® Healthy Real
   Egg Substitute**
**½ cup FLEISCHMANN'S® Original
   Margarine, melted**
¼ cup unsweetened cocoa
1½ teaspoons vanilla extract
**⅓ cup PLANTERS® Pecans, chopped
   Powdered sugar**

1. Mix flour, sugars, egg substitute, melted margarine and cocoa in large bowl until well blended. Stir in vanilla and pecans.

2. Spread in well greased 13×9×2-inch baking pan. Bake in preheated 350°F oven for 25 minutes or until done. Cool in pan on wire rack. Dust with powdered sugar; cut into bars. *Makes 3 dozen*

Preparation Time: 20 minutes
Cook Time: 25 minutes
Total Time: 45 minutes

Crimson Ribbon Bars

Triple Chocolate Brownies

3 squares (1 ounce *each*)
    unsweetened chocolate,
    coarsely chopped
2 squares (1 ounce *each*)
    semisweet chocolate, coarsely
    chopped
½ cup butter
1 cup all-purpose flour
½ teaspoon salt
¼ teaspoon baking powder
1½ cups sugar
3 eggs
1 teaspoon vanilla
¼ cup sour cream
½ cup milk chocolate chips
    Powdered sugar (optional)

Preheat oven to 350°F. Lightly grease 13×9-inch baking pan.

Place unsweetened chocolate, semisweet chocolate and butter in medium microwavable bowl. Microwave at HIGH 2 minutes or until butter is melted; stir until chocolate is completely melted. Cool to room temperature.

Combine flour, salt and baking powder in small bowl.

Beat sugar, eggs and vanilla in large bowl with electric mixer at medium speed until slightly thickened. Beat in chocolate mixture until well combined. Add flour mixture; beat at low speed until blended. Add sour cream; beat at low speed until combined. Stir in chocolate chips. Spread mixture evenly into prepared pan.

Bake 20 to 25 minutes or until toothpick inserted into center comes out almost clean. *Do not overbake.* Cool brownies

completely in pan on wire rack. Cut into 2-inch squares. Place powdered sugar in fine-mesh strainer; sprinkle over brownies, if desired. *Makes 2 dozen brownies*

Marshmallow Krispie Bars

1 package DUNCAN HINES® Fudge
    Brownie Mix, Family Size
1 package (10½ ounces) miniature
    marshmallows
1½ cups semi-sweet chocolate chips
1 cup creamy peanut butter
1 tablespoon butter or margarine
1½ cups crisp rice cereal

1. Preheat oven to 350°F. Grease bottom of 13×9-inch pan.

2. Prepare and bake brownies following package directions for basic recipe. Remove from oven. Sprinkle marshmallows on hot brownies. Return to oven. Bake for 3 minutes longer.

3. Place chocolate chips, peanut butter and butter in medium saucepan. Cook over low heat, stirring constantly, until chips are melted. Add rice cereal; mix well. Spread mixture over marshmallow layer. Refrigerate until chilled. Cut into bars. *Makes about 2 dozen bars*

Tip: For a special presentation, cut cookies into diamond shapes.

Triple Chocolate Brownies

Cookie Jar Classics

Peanut Butter Chocolate Chippers

1 cup creamy peanut butter
1 cup packed light brown sugar
1 egg
¾ cup milk chocolate chips
Granulated sugar

Preheat oven to 350°F. Combine peanut butter, sugar and egg in medium bowl; mix with spoon. Add chips; mix well. Roll heaping tablespoonfuls of dough into 1½-inch balls. Place balls 2 inches apart on ungreased cookie sheets. Dip fork into granulated sugar; press criss-cross fashion onto each ball, flattening to ½-inch thickness. Bake 12 minutes or until set. Let cookies stand on cookie sheets 2 minutes. Remove cookies with spatula to wire racks; cool completely. *Makes about 2 dozen cookies*

Note: This simple recipe is unusual because it doesn't contain any flour—but it still makes great cookies!

Chocolate Chips Thumbprint Cookies

  1 cup HERSHEY'S Semi-Sweet
    Chocolate Chips, divided
½ cup sugar
¼ cup butter flavor shortening
¼ cup (½ stick) butter or margarine,
    softened
  1 egg, separated
½ teaspoon vanilla extract
  1 cup all-purpose flour
¼ teaspoon salt
  1 cup finely chopped nuts

1. Heat oven to 350°F. Lightly grease cookie sheet. Place ¼ cup chocolate chips in small microwave-safe bowl. Microwave at HIGH (100%) 20 to 30 seconds or just until chocolate is melted and smooth when stirred; set aside to cool slightly.

2. Combine sugar, shortening, butter, reserved melted chocolate, egg yolk and vanilla; beat until well blended. Stir in flour and salt. Roll dough into 1-inch balls. With fork, slightly beat egg white. Dip each ball into egg white; roll in nuts to coat. Place about 1-inch apart on ungreased cookie sheet. Press center of each cookie with thumb to make indentation.

3. Bake 10 to 12 minutes or until set. Remove from oven; immediately place several chocolate chips in center of each cookie. Carefully remove from cookie sheet to wire rack. After several minutes, swirl melted chocolate in each thumbprint. Cool completely.

Makes about 2½ dozen cookies

Crispy Oat Drops

  1 cup (2 sticks) butter or margarine,
    softened
½ cup granulated sugar
½ cup firmly packed light brown
    sugar
  1 large egg
  2 cups all-purpose flour
½ cup quick-cooking or old-
    fashioned oats, uncooked
  1 teaspoon cream of tartar
½ teaspoon baking soda
¼ teaspoon salt
1¾ cups "M&M's"® Semi-Sweet
    Chocolate Mini Baking Bits
  1 cup toasted rice cereal
½ cup shredded coconut
½ cup coarsely chopped pecans

Preheat oven to 350°F. In large bowl cream butter and sugars until light and fluffy; beat in egg. In medium bowl combine flour, oats, cream of tartar, baking soda and salt; blend flour mixture into creamed mixture. Stir in "M&M's"® Semi-Sweet Chocolate Mini Baking Bits, cereal, coconut and pecans. Drop by heaping tablespoonfuls about 2 inches apart onto ungreased cookie sheets. Bake 10 to 13 minutes or until lightly browned. Cool completely on wire racks. Store in tightly covered container.

Makes about 4 dozen cookies

Crispy Oat Drops

Mocha Crinkles

1⅓ cups firmly packed light brown sugar
½ cup vegetable oil
¼ cup low-fat sour cream
1 egg
1 teaspoon vanilla
1¾ cups all-purpose flour
¾ cup unsweetened cocoa powder
2 teaspoons instant espresso or coffee granules
1 teaspoon baking soda
¼ teaspoon salt
⅛ teaspoon ground black pepper
½ cup powdered sugar

1. Beat brown sugar and oil in medium bowl with electric mixer. Mix in sour cream, egg and vanilla. Set aside.

2. Mix flour, cocoa, espresso, baking soda, salt and pepper in another medium bowl.

3. Add flour mixture to brown sugar mixture; mix well. Refrigerate dough until firm, 3 to 4 hours.

4. Preheat oven to 350°F. Pour powdered sugar into shallow bowl. Set aside. Cut dough into 1-inch pieces; roll into balls. Roll balls in powdered sugar.

5. Bake on ungreased cookie sheets 10 to 12 minutes or until tops of cookies are firm to touch. *Do not overbake.* Cool on wire racks.   *Makes 6 dozen cookies*

Peanut Gems

2½ cups all-purpose flour
1 teaspoon baking powder
⅛ teaspoon salt
1 cup butter, softened
1 cup packed light brown sugar
2 eggs
2 teaspoons vanilla
1½ cups cocktail peanuts, finely chopped
Powdered sugar (optional)

Preheat oven to 350°F. Combine flour, baking powder and salt in small bowl.

Beat butter in large bowl with electric mixer at medium speed until smooth. Gradually beat in brown sugar; increase speed to medium-high and beat until light and fluffy. Beat in eggs, 1 at a time, until fluffy. Beat in vanilla. Gradually stir in flour mixture until blended. Stir in peanuts until blended.

Drop heaping tablespoonfuls of dough about 1 inch apart onto ungreased cookie sheets; flatten slightly with hands.

Bake 12 minutes or until set. Let cookies stand on cookie sheets 5 minutes; transfer to wire racks to cool completely. Dust cookies with powdered sugar, if desired. Store in airtight container.
   Makes about 2½ dozen cookies

Mocha Crinkles

Almond Milk Chocolate Chippers

½ cup slivered almonds
1¼ cups all-purpose flour
½ teaspoon baking soda
½ teaspoon salt
½ cup butter or margarine, softened
½ cup firmly packed light brown sugar
⅓ cup granulated sugar
1 egg
2 tablespoons almond-flavored liqueur
1 cup milk chocolate chips

1. Preheat oven to 350°F. To toast almonds, spread on baking sheet. Bake 8 to 10 minutes or until golden brown, stirring frequently. Remove almonds from pan and cool; set aside.

2. *Increase oven temperature to 375°F.* Place flour, baking soda and salt in small bowl; stir to combine.

3. Beat butter, brown sugar and granulated sugar in large bowl with electric mixer at medium speed until light and fluffy. Beat in egg until well blended. Beat in liqueur. Gradually add flour mixture. Beat at low speed until well blended. Stir in chips and almonds with spoon.

4. Drop rounded teaspoonfuls of dough 2 inches apart onto ungreased cookie sheets.

5. Bake 9 to 10 minutes or until edges are golden brown. Let cookies stand on cookie sheets 2 minutes. Remove cookies with spatula to wire racks; cool completely.
Makes about 3 dozen cookies

Frosty's Colorful Cookies

1¼ cups firmly packed light brown sugar
¾ Butter Flavor* CRISCO® Stick or ¾ cup Butter Flavor CRISCO all-vegetable shortening
2 tablespoons milk
1 tablespoon vanilla
1 egg
1¾ cups all-purpose flour
1 teaspoon salt
¾ teaspoon baking soda
2 cups red and green candy-coated chocolate pieces

*Butter Flavor Crisco® is artificially flavored.

1. Heat oven to 375°F. Place sheets of foil on countertop for cooling cookies.

2. Place brown sugar, ¾ cup shortening, milk and vanilla in large bowl. Beat at medium speed of electric mixer until well blended. Add egg; beat well.

3. Combine flour, salt and baking soda. Add to shortening mixture; beat at low speed just until blended. Stir in candy-coated chocolate pieces.

4. Drop dough by rounded measuring tablespoonfuls 3 inches apart onto ungreased baking sheets.

5. Bake one baking sheet at a time at 375°F for 8 to 10 minutes for chewy cookies, or 11 to 13 minutes for crisp cookies. *Do not overbake.* Cool 2 minutes on baking sheet. Remove cookies to foil to cool completely.
Makes about 3 dozen cookies

Almond Milk Chocolate Chippers

Hershey's Great American Chocolate Chip Cookies

1 cup (2 sticks) butter, softened
¾ cup granulated sugar
¾ cup packed light brown sugar
1 teaspoon vanilla extract
2 eggs
2¼ cups all-purpose flour
1 teaspoon baking soda
½ teaspoon salt
2 cups (12-ounce package) HERSHEY'S Semi-Sweet Chocolate Chips
1 cup chopped nuts (optional)

Heat oven to 375°F. Beat butter, granulated sugar, brown sugar and vanilla in large bowl until creamy. Add eggs; beat well. Stir together flour, baking soda and salt; gradually add to butter mixture, beating well. Stir in chocolate chips and nuts, if desired. Drop dough by rounded teaspoonfuls onto ungreased cookie sheet. Bake 8 to 10 minutes or until lightly browned. Cool slightly; remove from cookie sheet to wire rack. Cool completely.

Makes about 6 dozen cookies

Hershey's Great American Chocolate Chip Pan Cookies: Spread dough into greased 15½×10½×1-inch jelly-roll pan. Bake at 375°F 20 minutes or until lightly browned. Cool completely in pan on wire rack. Makes about 4 dozen bars.

Skor® & Chocolate Chip Cookies: Omit 1 cup HERSHEY'S Semi-Sweet Chocolate Chips and nuts; replace with 1 cup finely chopped SKOR® bars. Drop onto cookie sheets and bake as directed.

Great American Ice Cream Sandwiches: Prepare cookies as directed. Place one small scoop slightly softened vanilla ice cream between flat sides of two cookies. Gently press together. Wrap and freeze.

Spicy Oatmeal Raisin Cookies

1 package DUNCAN HINES® Moist Deluxe Spice Cake Mix
4 egg whites
1 cup quick-cooking oats (not instant or old-fashioned), uncooked
½ cup canola oil
½ cup raisins

1. Preheat oven to 350°F. Grease cookie sheets.

2. Combine cake mix, egg whites, oats and oil in large mixer bowl. Beat on low speed with electric mixer until blended. Stir in raisins. Drop by rounded teaspoons onto prepared cookie sheets.

3. Bake 7 to 9 minutes or until lightly browned. Cool 1 minute on cookie sheets. Remove to cooling racks; cool completely.

Makes about 4 dozen cookies

Ultimate Chippers

2½ cups all-purpose flour
1 teaspoon baking soda
½ teaspoon salt
1 cup butter or margarine, softened
1 cup packed light brown sugar
½ cup granulated sugar
2 eggs
1 tablespoon vanilla
1 cup semisweet chocolate chips
1 cup milk chocolate chips
1 cup vanilla milk chips
½ cup coarsely chopped pecans
   (optional)

Preheat oven to 375°F. Combine flour, baking soda and salt in medium bowl.

Beat butter, brown sugar and granulated sugar in large bowl until light and fluffy. Beat in eggs and vanilla. Add flour mixture to butter mixture; beat until well blended. Stir in chips and pecans, if desired.

Drop by heaping teaspoonfuls 2 inches apart onto ungreased cookie sheets. Bake 10 to 12 minutes or until edges are golden brown. Let cookies stand on cookie sheets 2 minutes. Remove cookies to wire racks; cool completely.

Makes about 6 dozen cookies

Molasses Spice Cookies

1 cup granulated sugar
¾ cup shortening
¼ cup molasses
1 egg, beaten
2 cups all-purpose flour
2 teaspoons baking soda
1 teaspoon ground cinnamon
1 teaspoon ground cloves
1 teaspoon ground ginger
¼ teaspoon dry mustard
¼ teaspoon salt
½ cup granulated brown sugar

1. Preheat oven to 375°F. Grease cookie sheets; set aside.

2. Beat granulated sugar and shortening about 5 minutes in large bowl until light and fluffy. Add molasses and egg; beat until fluffy.

3. Combine flour, baking soda, cinnamon, cloves, ginger, mustard and salt in medium bowl. Add to shortening mixture; mix until just combined.

4. Place brown sugar in shallow dish. Roll tablespoonfuls of dough into 1-inch balls; roll in sugar to coat. Place 2 inches apart on prepared cookie sheets. Bake 15 minutes or until lightly browned. Let cookies stand on cookie sheets 2 minutes. Remove cookies to wire racks; cool completely.

Makes about 6 dozen cookies

Two-Toned Spritz Cookies

1 square (1 ounce) unsweetened chocolate, coarsely chopped
1 cup (2 sticks) butter or margarine, softened
1 cup sugar
1 egg
1 teaspoon vanilla
2¼ cups all-purpose flour
¼ teaspoon salt

Melt chocolate in small heavy saucepan over low heat, stirring constantly; set aside. Beat butter and sugar in large bowl until light and fluffy. Beat in egg and vanilla. Combine flour and salt in medium bowl; gradually add to butter mixture. Reserve 2 cups dough. Beat chocolate into dough in bowl until smooth. Cover both doughs and refrigerate until firm enough to handle, about 20 minutes.

Preheat oven to 400°F. Roll out vanilla dough between two sheets of waxed paper to ½-inch thickness. Cut into 5×4-inch rectangles. Place chocolate dough on sheet of waxed paper. Using waxed paper to hold dough, roll back and forth to form a log about 1 inch in diameter. Cut into 5-inch-long logs. Place chocolate log in center of vanilla rectangle. Wrap vanilla dough around log and fit into cookie press fitted with star disc. Press dough onto ungreased cookie sheets 1½ inches apart. Bake about 10 minutes or until just set. Remove cookies with spatula to wire racks; cool completely.
Makes about 4 dozen cookies

Double Nut Chocolate Chip Cookies

1 package DUNCAN HINES® Moist Deluxe Yellow Cake Mix
½ cup butter or margarine, melted
1 egg
1 cup semisweet chocolate chips
½ cup finely chopped pecans
1 cup sliced almonds, divided

1. Preheat oven to 375°F. Grease cookie sheets.

2. Combine cake mix, butter and egg in large bowl. Mix at low speed with electric mixer until just blended. Stir in chocolate chips, pecans and ¼ cup almonds. Shape rounded tablespoonfuls of dough into balls. Place remaining ¾ cup almonds in shallow bowl. Press tops of cookies in almonds. Place 1 inch apart on prepared cookie sheets.

3. Bake 9 to 11 minutes or until lightly browned. Cool 2 minutes on cookie sheets. Remove to cooling racks.
Makes 3 to 3½ dozen cookies

Two-Toned Spritz Cookies

Maple Walnut Meringues

⅓ cup powdered sugar
½ cup plus ⅓ cup ground walnuts, divided
¾ cup packed light brown sugar
3 egg whites, at room temperature
  Pinch salt
⅛ teaspoon cream of tartar
1 teaspoon maple extract

Place 1 oven rack in the top third of oven and 1 oven rack in the bottom third of oven. Preheat oven to 300°F. Line 2 large cookie sheets with foil, shiny side up. Stir powdered sugar and ½ cup walnuts with fork in medium bowl; set aside. Crumble brown sugar into small bowl; set aside. Beat egg whites and salt in large bowl with electric mixer at high speed until foamy. Add cream of tartar; beat 30 seconds or until mixture forms soft peaks. Sprinkle brown sugar 1 tablespoon at a time over egg white mixture; beat at high speed until each addition is completely absorbed. Beat 2 to 3 minutes or until mixture forms stiff peaks. Beat in maple extract at low speed. Fold in walnut mixture with large rubber spatula. Drop level tablespoonfuls of dough to form mounds about 1 inch apart on prepared cookie sheets. Sprinkle cookies with remaining ⅓ cup ground walnuts. Bake 25 minutes or until cookies feel dry on surface but remain soft inside. (Rotate cookie sheets from top to bottom halfway through baking time.) Slide foil with cookies onto wire racks; cool completely. Carefully remove cookies from foil. Store in airtight container with wax paper between layers of cookies. Cookies are best the day they are baked.
Makes about 3 dozen cookies

Chocolate Drop Sugar Cookies

⅔ cup butter or margarine, softened
1 cup sugar
1 egg
1½ teaspoons vanilla extract
1½ cups all-purpose flour
½ cup HERSHEY'S Cocoa
½ teaspoon baking soda
¼ teaspoon salt
⅓ cup buttermilk or sour milk*
  Additional sugar

*To sour milk: Use 1 teaspoon white vinegar plus milk to equal ⅓ cup.

1. Heat oven to 350°F. Lightly grease cookie sheet.

2. Beat butter and sugar in large bowl until well blended. Add egg and vanilla; beat until light and fluffy. Stir together flour, cocoa, baking soda and salt; add alternately with buttermilk to butter mixture. Using ice cream scoop or ¼ cup measuring cup, drop dough about 2 inches apart onto prepared cookie sheet.

3. Bake 13 to 15 minutes or until cookie springs back when touched lightly in center. While cookies are on cookie sheet, sprinkle lightly with additional sugar. Cool slightly; remove from cookie sheet to wire rack. Cool completely.
Makes about 1 dozen cookies

Maple Walnut Meringues

Oatmeal Raisin Cookies

¾ cup all-purpose flour
¾ teaspoon salt
½ teaspoon baking soda
½ teaspoon ground cinnamon
¾ cup butter or margarine, softened
¾ cup granulated sugar
¾ cup packed light brown sugar
1 egg
1 tablespoon water
3 teaspoons vanilla, divided
3 cups uncooked quick-cooking or
    old-fashioned oats
1 cup raisins
½ cup powdered sugar
1 tablespoon milk

Preheat oven to 375°F. Grease cookie sheets; set aside. Combine flour, salt, baking soda and cinnamon in small bowl.

Beat butter, granulated sugar and brown sugar in large bowl with electric mixer at medium speed until light and fluffy. Add egg, water and 2 teaspoons vanilla; beat well. Add flour mixture; beat at low speed just until blended. Stir in oats with spoon. Stir in raisins.

Drop tablespoonfuls of dough 2 inches apart onto prepared cookie sheets.

Bake 10 to 11 minutes or until edges are golden brown. Let cookies stand 2 minutes on cookie sheets; transfer to wire racks to cool completely.

For glaze, stir powdered sugar, milk and remaining 1 teaspoon vanilla in small bowl until smooth. Drizzle over cookies with fork or spoon.
Makes about 4 dozen cookies

Cocoa Nut Bundles

1 can (8 ounces) refrigerated quick
    crescent dinner rolls
2 tablespoons butter or margarine,
    softened
1 tablespoon granulated sugar
2 teaspoons HERSHEY'S Cocoa
¼ cup chopped nuts
    Powdered sugar

1. Heat oven to 375°F. Unroll dough and separate to form 8 triangles on ungreased cookie sheet.

2. Combine butter, granulated sugar and cocoa in small bowl. Add nuts; mix thoroughly. Divide chocolate mixture evenly among triangles, placing on wide end of triangle. Take dough on either side of mixture and pull up and over mixture, tucking ends under. Continue rolling dough toward opposite point.

3. Bake 9 to 10 minutes or until golden brown. Sprinkle with powdered sugar; serve warm.
Makes 8 rolls

Oatmeal Raisin Cookies

Chocolate Bonanza

Festive Fudge Blossoms

1 box (18.25 ounces) chocolate fudge cake
   mix
¼ cup butter or margarine, softened
1 egg, slightly beaten
¾ to 1 cup finely chopped walnuts
48 chocolate star candies

Preheat oven to 350°F. Cut butter into cake mix
in large bowl until coarse crumbs form. Stir in egg
and 2 tablespoons water until well blended. Shape
dough into ½-inch balls; roll in walnuts, pressing nuts
gently into dough. Place about 2 inches apart onto
ungreased baking sheets. Bake cookies 12 minutes
or until puffed and nearly set. Place chocolate star
in center of each cookie; bake 1 minute. Cool 2
minutes on baking sheet. Remove cookies from
baking sheets to wire rack to cool completely.

Makes 4 dozen cookies

Czech Bear Paws

4 cups toasted ground hazelnuts
2 cups all-purpose flour
1 tablespoon unsweetened cocoa
**   powder**
1 teaspoon ground cinnamon
½ teaspoon ground nutmeg
¼ teaspoon salt
1 cup butter plus 3 teaspoons
**   butter, softened, divided**
1 cup powdered sugar
1 egg yolk
½ cup melted chocolate chips
**   Slivered almonds, halved**

1. Preheat oven to 350°F. Place hazelnuts, flour, cocoa, cinnamon, nutmeg and salt in medium bowl; stir to combine.

2. Beat 1 cup butter, powdered sugar and egg yolk in large bowl with electric mixer at medium speed until light and fluffy. Gradually add flour mixture. Beat at low speed until soft dough forms.

3. Grease 3 madeleine pans with remaining softened butter, 1 teaspoon per pan; dust with flour. (If only 1 madeleine pan is available, thoroughly wash, dry, regrease and flour after baking each batch. Cover remaining dough with plastic wrap; let stand at room temperature.) Press level tablespoonfuls of dough into each mold.

4. Bake 12 minutes or until lightly browned. Let cookies stand in pan 3 minutes. Carefully loosen cookies from pan with point of small knife. Invert pan over wire racks; tap lightly to release cookies. Let stand 2 minutes. Turn cookies shell-side up; cool completely.

5. Pipe squiggle of melted chocolate on curved end of each cookie; place slivered almond halves in melted chocolate for claws. Let stand at room temperature 1 hour or until set. Store tightly covered at room temperature.

Makes about 5 dozen cookies

Note: These cookies do not freeze well.

Triple Chocolate Cookies

1 package DUNCAN HINES® Moist
**   Deluxe® Swiss Chocolate Cake**
**   Mix**
½ cup butter or margarine, melted
1 egg
½ cup semi-sweet chocolate chips
½ cup milk chocolate chips
½ cup coarsely chopped white
**   chocolate**
½ cup chopped pecans

1. Preheat oven to 375°F.

2. Combine cake mix, melted butter and egg in large bowl. Beat at low speed with electric mixer until blended. Stir in all 3 chocolates and pecans.

3. Drop by rounded tablespoonfuls onto ungreased baking sheets. Bake at 375°F 9 to 11 minutes. Cool 1 minute on baking sheet. Remove to cooling racks.

Makes 3½ to 4 dozen cookies

Tip: Cookies may be stored in an airtight container in freezer for up to 6 months.

Czech Bear Paws

Chocolate Peanut Butter Cup Cookies

Cookies

1 cup semi-sweet chocolate chips
**2 squares (1 ounce each)
    unsweetened baking chocolate**
1 cup sugar
**½ Butter Flavor* CRISCO® Stick or
    ½ cup Butter Flavor CRISCO®
    all-vegetable shortening**
2 eggs
1 teaspoon salt
1 teaspoon vanilla
**1½ cups plus 2 tablespoons
    all-purpose flour**
½ teaspoon baking soda
¾ cup finely chopped peanuts
**36 miniature peanut butter cups,
    unwrapped**

Drizzle

1 cup peanut butter chips

*Butter Flavor Crisco® is artificially flavored.

1. Heat oven to 350°F. Place sheets of foil on countertop for cooling cookies.

2. For cookies, combine chocolate chips and chocolate squares in microwave-safe measuring cup or bowl. Microwave at 50% (MEDIUM). Stir after 2 minutes. Repeat until smooth (or melt on rangetop in small saucepan on very low heat). Cool slightly.

3. Combine sugar and ½ cup shortening in large bowl. Beat at medium speed of electric mixer until blended and crumbly. Beat in eggs, one at a time, then salt and vanilla. Reduce speed to low. Add chocolate slowly. Mix until well blended. Stir in flour and baking soda with spoon until well blended. Shape dough into 1¼-inch balls. Roll in nuts. Place 2 inches apart on ungreased baking sheet.

4. Bake at 350°F for 8 to 10 minutes or until set. *Do not overbake.* Press peanut butter cup into center of each cookie immediately. Press cookie against cup. Cool 2 minutes on baking sheet before removing to cooling rack. Cool completely.

5. For drizzle, place peanut butter chips in heavy resealable sandwich bag. Seal. Microwave at 50% (MEDIUM). Knead bag after 1 minute. Repeat until smooth (or melt by placing bag in hot water). Cut tiny tip off corner of bag. Squeeze out and drizzle over cookies.

Makes 3 dozen cookies

Helpful Hint

Chocolate should be stored in a cool, dry place (60°F to 70°F) to avoid the appearance of "bloom," a gray-white film on the surface.

Chocolate Peanut Butter Cup Cookies

Triple Chocolate Pretzels

2 squares (1 ounce *each*)
 unsweetened chocolate
½ cup butter or margarine, softened
½ cup granulated sugar
1 egg
2 cups cake flour
1 teaspoon vanilla
¼ teaspoon salt
 Mocha Glaze (recipe follows)
2 ounces white chocolate, chopped

Melt unsweetened chocolate in top of double boiler over hot, not boiling, water. Remove from heat; cool. Beat butter and granulated sugar in large bowl until light. Add egg and melted chocolate; beat until fluffy. Stir in cake flour, vanilla and salt until well blended. Cover; refrigerate until firm, about 1 hour.

Preheat oven to 400°F. Lightly grease cookie sheets or line with parchment paper. Divide dough into 4 equal parts. Divide each part into 12 pieces. To form pretzels, knead each piece briefly to soften dough. Roll into a rope about 6 inches long. Form each rope on prepared cookie sheet into a pretzel shape. Repeat with all pieces of dough, spacing cookies 2 inches apart.

Bake 7 to 9 minutes or until firm. Remove to wire racks to cool. Prepare Mocha Glaze. Dip pretzels into glaze to coat completely. Place on waxed paper, right side up. Let stand until glaze is set.

Melt white chocolate in small bowl over hot water. Squeeze melted chocolate through pastry bag or drizzle over pretzels to decorate. Let stand until chocolate is completely set.

Makes 4 dozen cookies

Mocha Glaze

1 cup (6 ounces) semisweet
 chocolate chips
1 teaspoon light corn syrup
1 teaspoon shortening
1 cup powdered sugar
3 to 5 tablespoons hot coffee or
 water

Combine chocolate chips, corn syrup and shortening in small heavy saucepan. Stir over low heat until chocolate is melted. Stir in powdered sugar and enough coffee to make a smooth glaze.

Helpful Hint

For even baking and browning, place only one cookie sheet at a time in the center of the oven. If the cookies brown unevenly, rotate the cookie sheet from front to back halfway through the baking time.

Chocolate Sugar Spritz

2 squares (1 ounce *each*)
    unsweetened chocolate,
    coarsely chopped
2¼ cups all-purpose flour
¼ teaspoon salt
1 cup butter or margarine, softened
¾ cup granulated sugar
1 egg
1 teaspoon almond extract
½ cup powdered sugar
1 teaspoon ground cinnamon

1. Preheat oven to 400°F.

2. Melt chocolate in small heavy saucepan over low heat, stirring constantly; set aside.

3. Combine flour and salt in small bowl; stir to combine.

4. Beat butter and granulated sugar in large bowl with electric mixer at medium speed until light and fluffy. Beat in egg and almond extract. Beat in chocolate. Gradually add flour mixture with mixing spoon. (Dough will be stiff.)

5. Fit cookie press with desired plate (or change plates for different shapes after first batch). Fill press with dough; press dough 1 inch apart onto ungreased cookie sheets. Bake 7 minutes or until just set.

6. Combine powdered sugar and cinnamon in small bowl. Transfer to fine-mesh strainer and sprinkle over hot cookies while they are still on cookie sheets. Remove cookies with spatula to wire racks; cool completely. Store tightly covered at room temperature.

Makes 4 to 5 dozen cookies

Caramel Nut Chocolate Cookies

1½ cups firmly packed light brown
    sugar
⅔ CRISCO® Stick or ⅔ cup CRISCO®
    all-vegetable shortening
1 tablespoon water
1 teaspoon vanilla
2 eggs
1¾ cups all-purpose flour
⅓ cup unsweetened cocoa powder
½ teaspoon salt
¼ teaspoon baking soda
2 cups (12 ounces) miniature
    semisweet chocolate chips
1 cup chopped pecans
20 to 25 caramels, unwrapped and
    halved

1. Heat oven to 375°F. Place sheets of foil on countertop for cooling cookies.

2. Place brown sugar, shortening, water and vanilla in large bowl. Beat at medium speed of electric mixer until well blended. Add eggs; beat well.

3. Combine flour, cocoa, salt and baking soda. Add to shortening mixture; beat at low speed just until blended. Stir in small chocolate chips.

4. Shape dough into 1¼-inch balls. Dip tops in chopped pecans. Place 2 inches apart on ungreased baking sheet. Press caramel half in center of each ball.

5. Bake one baking sheet at a time at 375°F for 7 to 9 minutes or until cookies are set. *Do not overbake.* Cool 2 minutes on baking sheet. Remove cookies to foil to cool completely.

Makes about 4 dozen cookies

S'more Snack Treats

**44 squares HONEY MAID® Honey
    Grahams (2 sleeves)**
**3 tablespoons FLEISCHMANN'S®
    Original Margarine**
**1 (10-ounce) package
    marshmallows**
**¾ cup miniature semisweet
    chocolate chips**

1. Break grahams into bite-size pieces;
set aside.

2. Heat margarine in large saucepan
over medium heat until melted. Add
marshmallows, stirring constantly until
melted.

3. Stir broken crackers into marshmallow
mixture to coat evenly. Spread mixture
into lightly greased 13×9×2-inch pan;
sprinkle with chocolate chips, pressing
lightly with greased hands.

4. Chill at least 20 minutes before cutting
into squares.   *Makes 12 s'mores*

Preparation Time: 15 minutes

Cook Time: 20 minutes

Chill Time: 20 minutes

Total Time: 55 minutes

Festive Chocolate Chip Cookies

**1 package DUNCAN HINES® Moist
    Deluxe® White Cake Mix**
**¼ cup firmly packed light brown
    sugar**
1 egg
¾ cup vegetable oil
**1 package (6 ounces) semi-sweet
    chocolate chips**
½ cup chopped pecans or walnuts
Assorted decors

1. Preheat oven to 350°F.

2. Combine cake mix, brown sugar, egg
and oil in large bowl. Beat at low speed
with electric mixer until blended. Stir in
chocolate chips and pecans. Form dough
into 1½-inch ball. Dip top of ball in decors.
Place ball decor-side up on ungreased
baking sheets. Repeat with remaining
dough placing balls 2 inches apart on
baking sheets. Bake at 350°F 10 to
12 minutes or until light golden brown
around edges. Cool 2 minutes on baking
sheets. Remove to cooling racks. Cool
completely. Store in airtight container.
            Makes 3 to 3½ dozen cookies

Tip: Cool baking sheet completely before
baking each batch of cookies.

S'more Snack Treats

Marshmallow Sandwich Cookies

⅔ **cup butter**
1¼ **cups sugar**
¼ **cup light corn syrup**
1 **egg**
1 **teaspoon vanilla**
2 **cups all-purpose flour**
½ **cup unsweetened cocoa powder**
2 **teaspoons baking soda**
¼ **teaspoon salt**
Sugar for rolling
24 **large marshmallows**

Preheat oven to 350°F. Beat butter and 1¼ cups sugar in large bowl until light and fluffy. Beat in corn syrup, egg and vanilla. Combine flour, cocoa, baking soda and salt in medium bowl; add to butter mixture. Beat until well blended. Cover and refrigerate dough 15 minutes or until firm enough to roll into balls.

Place sugar in shallow dish. Roll tablespoonfuls of dough into 1-inch balls; roll in sugar to coat. Place cookies 3 inches apart on ungreased cookie sheets. Bake 10 to 12 minutes or until set. Remove cookies to wire rack; cool completely.

To assemble sandwiches, place one marshmallow on flat side of one cookie on paper plate. Microwave at HIGH 12 seconds or until marshmallow just begins to melt. Immediately place another cookie, flat side down, on top of hot marshmallow; press together slightly.

Makes about 2 dozen sandwich cookies

Santa's Chocolate Cookies

1 **cup margarine or butter**
⅔ **cup semisweet chocolate chips**
¾ **cup sugar**
1 **egg**
½ **teaspoon vanilla**
2 **cups all-purpose flour**
Apricot jam, melted semisweet chocolate, chopped almonds, frosting, coconut or colored sprinkles

Preheat oven to 350°F. Melt margarine and chocolate together in small saucepan over low heat or microwave 2 minutes at HIGH until completely melted. Combine chocolate mixture and sugar in large bowl. Add egg and vanilla; stir well. Add flour; stir well. Refrigerate 30 minutes or until firm.

Shape dough into 1-inch balls. Place 1 inch apart on ungreased cookie sheets. If desired, flatten balls with bottom of drinking glass, shape into logs or make a depression in center and fill with apricot jam.

Bake 8 to 10 minutes or until set. Remove to wire racks to cool completely. Decorate as desired with melted chocolate, almonds, frosting, coconut and colored sprinkles.

Makes about 3 dozen cookies

Marshmallow Sandwich Cookies

Nutty Clusters

**2 squares (1 ounce *each*)
  unsweetened chocolate
½ cup butter or margarine, softened
1 cup granulated sugar
1 egg
⅓ cup buttermilk
1 teaspoon vanilla
1¾ cups all-purpose flour
½ teaspoon baking soda
1 cup mixed salted nuts, chopped
  Easy Chocolate Icing
  (recipe follows)**

Preheat oven to 400°F. Line cookie sheets with parchment paper or leave ungreased. Melt chocolate in top of double boiler over hot, not boiling, water. Remove from heat; cool. Beat butter and granulated sugar in large bowl until smooth. Beat in egg, melted chocolate, buttermilk and vanilla until light. Stir in flour, baking soda and nuts. Drop dough by teaspoonfuls 2 inches apart onto cookie sheets. Bake 8 to 10 minutes or until almost no imprint remains when touched. Immediately remove cookies from cookie sheets to wire racks. While cookies bake, prepare Easy Chocolate Icing. Frost cookies while still warm.

Makes about 4 dozen cookies

Easy Chocolate Icing

**2 squares (1 ounce *each*)
  unsweetened chocolate
2 tablespoons butter or margarine
2 cups powdered sugar
2 to 3 tablespoons water**

Melt chocolate and butter in small heavy saucepan over low heat, stirring until completely melted. Add powdered sugar and water, mixing until smooth.

Chocolate Macaroons

**1 can (8 ounces) almond paste
½ cup powdered sugar
2 egg whites
12 ounces semisweet baking
  chocolate or chips, melted
2 tablespoons all-purpose flour
  Powdered sugar (optional)**

Preheat oven to 300°F. Line cookie sheets with parchment paper; set aside.

Beat almond paste, sugar and egg whites in large bowl with electric mixer at medium speed 1 minute. Beat in chocolate until well combined. Beat in flour at low speed.

Spoon dough into pastry bag fitted with rosette tip. Pipe 1½-inch spirals 1 inch apart onto prepared cookie sheets. Pipe all cookies at once; dough will get stiff upon standing.

Bake 20 minutes or until set. Carefully remove parchment paper to countertop; cool completely.

Peel cookies off parchment paper. Sprinkle powdered sugar over cookies, if desired.

Makes about 3 dozen cookies

Nutty Clusters

Holiday Favorites

Candy Cane Cookies

1 cup sugar
⅔ cup FLEISCHMANN'S® Original Margarine, softened
½ cup EGG BEATERS® Healthy Real Egg Substitute
2 teaspoons vanilla extract
1 teaspoon almond extract
3 cups all-purpose flour
1 teaspoon DAVIS® Baking Powder
½ teaspoon red food coloring

1. Beat sugar and margarine in large bowl with mixer at medium speed until creamy. Beat in egg substitute, vanilla and almond extracts. Mix flour and baking powder; stir into margarine mixture.

continued on page 56

54

Candy Cane Cookies, continued

2. Divide dough in half; tint half with red food coloring. Wrap each half and refrigerate at least 2 hours.

3. Divide each half into 32 pieces. Roll each piece into a 5-inch rope. Twist 1 red and 1 white rope together and bend 1 end to form candy cane shape. Place on ungreased baking sheets.

4. Bake in preheated 350°F oven for 8 to 10 minutes or just until set and lightly golden. Remove from sheets; cool on wire racks. Store in airtight container.

Makes 32 cookies

Helpful Hint

Looking for something different to take to all your holiday gatherings? Decorate a metal tin with rubber stamps for a crafty look and fill it with candy cane cookies and an assortment of flavored coffees. Perfect for a "homey" hostess gift.

Cocoa Kiss Cookies

1 cup (2 sticks) butter or margarine, softened
⅔ cup sugar
1 teaspoon vanilla extract
1⅔ cups all-purpose flour
¼ cup HERSHEY'S Cocoa
1 cup finely chopped pecans
1 bag (9 ounces) HERSHEY'S KISSES® Milk Chocolates
Powdered sugar

1. Beat butter, sugar and vanilla in large bowl until creamy. Stir together flour and cocoa; gradually add to butter mixture, beating until blended. Add pecans; beat until well blended. Refrigerate dough about 1 hour or until firm enough to handle.

2. Heat oven to 375°F. Remove wrappers from chocolate pieces. Mold scant tablespoon of dough around each chocolate piece, covering completely. Shape into balls. Place on ungreased cookie sheet.

3. Bake 10 to 12 minutes or until set. Cool slightly, about 1 minute; remove from cookie sheet to wire rack. Cool completely. Roll in powdered sugar. Roll in sugar again just before serving, if desired.

Makes about 4½ dozen cookies

Top to bottom: Cocoa Kiss Cookies and Hershey's Great American Chocolate Chip Cookies (page 32)

Slice 'n' Bake Ginger Wafers

½ cup butter or margarine, softened
1 cup packed brown sugar
¼ cup light molasses
1 egg
2 teaspoons ground ginger
1 teaspoon grated orange peel
¼ teaspoon salt
¼ teaspoon ground cinnamon
¼ teaspoon ground cloves
2 cups all-purpose flour

1. Beat butter, sugar and molasses in large bowl until light and fluffy. Add egg, ginger, orange peel, salt, cinnamon and cloves; beat until well blended. Stir in flour until well blended. (Dough will be very stiff.)

2. Divide dough in half. Roll each half into 8×1½-inch log. Wrap logs in waxed paper or plastic wrap; refrigerate at least 5 hours or up to 3 days.

3. Preheat oven to 350°F. Cut dough into ¼-inch-thick slices. Place about 2 inches apart on ungreased baking sheets. Bake 12 to 14 minutes or until set. Remove from baking sheet to wire rack to cool.
Makes about 4½ dozen cookies

Serving Suggestion: Dip half of each cookie in melted white chocolate or drizzle cookies with a glaze of 1¼ cups powdered sugar and 2 tablespoons orange juice. Or, cut cookie dough into ⅛-inch-thick slices; bake and sandwich melted caramel candy or peanut butter between cookies.

Snowball Cookies

1 cup margarine or butter, softened
1 cup sugar
1 teaspoon vanilla extract
2 cups all-purpose flour
1½ cups PLANTERS® Pecans, finely ground
¼ teaspoon salt
½ cup powdered sugar

1. Beat margarine, sugar and vanilla in large bowl with mixer at medium speed until creamy. Blend in flour, pecans and salt. Refrigerate 1 hour.

2. Shape dough into 1-inch balls. Place on ungreased baking sheets, 2 inches apart. Bake in preheated 350°F oven for 10 to 12 minutes. Remove from sheets; cool on wire racks. Dust with powdered sugar. Store in airtight container.
Makes 6 dozen cookies

Preparation Time: 15 minutes

Chill Time: 1 hour

Cook Time: 10 minutes

Total Time: 1 hour and 25 minutes

Slice 'n' Bake Ginger Wafers

Rum Fruitcake Cookies

 1 cup sugar
 ¾ cup vegetable shortening
 3 eggs
 ⅓ cup orange juice
 1 tablespoon rum extract
 3 cups all-purpose flour
 2 teaspoons baking powder
 1 teaspoon baking soda
 1 teaspoon salt
 2 cups (8 ounces) candied fruit
 1 cup raisins
 1 cup nuts, coarsely chopped

1. Preheat oven to 375°F. Lightly grease cookie sheets; set aside. Beat sugar and shortening in large bowl until fluffy. Add eggs, orange juice and rum extract; beat 2 minutes longer.

2. Combine flour, baking powder, baking soda and salt in small bowl. Add fruit, raisins and nuts. Stir into creamed mixture. Drop dough by rounded teaspoonfuls 2 inches apart onto prepared cookie sheets. Bake 10 to 12 minutes or until golden. Let cookies stand on cookie sheets 2 minutes. Remove to wire rack; cool completely.

Makes about 6 dozen cookies

Holiday Wreath Cookies

 1 package (20 ounces) refrigerated
    sugar cookie dough
 2 cups shredded coconut
 2 to 3 drops green food color
 1 container (16 ounces) ready-to-
    spread French vanilla frosting
   Green sugar or small cinnamon
    candies

1. Preheat oven to 350°F. Divide cookie dough in half (keep half of dough refrigerated until needed). Roll dough out on well-floured surface to ⅛-inch-thick rectangle. Cut with cookie cutters to resemble wreaths. Repeat with remaining half of dough.

2. Place cookies about 2 inches apart on ungreased baking sheets. Bake 7 to 9 minutes or until edges are lightly browned. Remove cookies from baking sheets to wire rack to cool completely.

3. Place coconut in resealable plastic food storage bag. Add food color; seal bag and shake until coconut is evenly colored. Frost cookies with frosting and decorate with coconut or green sugar and cinnamon candies.

Makes about 2 dozen cookies

Prep and Bake Time: 30 minutes

Rum Fruitcake Cookies

Pinecone Cookies

6 tablespoons butter or margarine
⅓ cup HERSHEY'S Cocoa or HERSHEY'S Dutch Processed Cocoa
1 cup sugar
2 eggs
1 teaspoon vanilla extract
2 cups all-purpose flour
½ teaspoon baking powder
½ teaspoon salt
¼ teaspoon baking soda
   Light corn syrup
   Sliced almonds

1. Melt butter in small saucepan; remove from heat. Add cocoa; blend well. Combine sugar, eggs, and vanilla in large bowl; blend in chocolate mixture. Stir together flour, baking powder, salt and baking soda; add to chocolate-sugar mixture, beating until smooth. Refrigerate dough about 1 hour or until firm enough to roll.

2. Heat oven to 350°F. Roll small portion of dough at a time between pieces of wax paper to ⅛-inch thickness. Cut into pinecone shapes using 2- or 2½-inch oval cookie cutter. Place on lightly greased cookie sheet; lightly brush cookies with corn syrup. Arrange almonds in pinecone fashion; lightly drizzle or brush almonds with corn syrup.

3. Bake 7 to 8 minutes or until set. Cool slightly; remove from cookie sheet to wire rack. Cool completely.
Makes about 4 dozen cookies

Holiday Sugar Cookies

2 cups all-purpose flour
½ teaspoon baking soda
1 cup FLEISCHMANN'S® Original Margarine, softened
1 cup plus 2 tablespoons sugar, divided
1 teaspoon vanilla extract
¼ cup EGG BEATERS® Healthy Real Egg Substitute

1. Mix flour and baking soda in small bowl; set aside.

2. Beat margarine, 1 cup sugar and vanilla in large bowl with mixer at medium speed until creamy. Beat in egg substitute until light and fluffy. Gradually blend in flour mixture. Wrap; refrigerate 4 hours.

3. Shape rounded teaspoons of dough into balls using floured hands. Place 2 inches apart on ungreased baking sheets. Grease bottom of small glass; dip in remaining sugar. Press balls to flatten slightly, dipping glass in remaining sugar as necessary.

4. Bake in preheated 375°F oven for 8 to 10 minutes. Remove from sheets; cool completely on wire racks.
Makes 4½ dozen cookies

Preparation Time: 15 minutes

Chill Time: 4 hours

Cook Time: 8 minutes

Total Time: 4 hours and 23 minutes

Peanut Butter Brickle Cookies

1½ cups all-purpose flour
1 cup granulated sugar
2 tablespoons packed light brown
    sugar
1 cup butter or margarine, softened
½ cup peanut butter
1 egg
½ teaspoon baking soda
1 teaspoon vanilla
1 package (6 ounces) almond
    brickle bits

Preheat oven to 350°F. Grease cookie sheets. Combine flour, granulated sugar, brown sugar, butter, peanut butter, egg, baking soda and vanilla in large bowl. Beat at medium speed of electric mixer until well blended, 2 to 3 minutes. Stir in almond brickle bits.

Shape rounded teaspoonfuls of dough into 1-inch balls. Place 2 inches apart on prepared cookie sheets. Flatten cookies to ⅛-inch thickness with bottom of glass covered with waxed paper. Bake 7 to 9 minutes or until edges are very lightly browned.

Makes about 4 dozen cookies

Scrumptious Chocolate Fruit and Nut Cookies

1¼ cups butter or margarine,
    softened
2 cups sugar
2 eggs
2 teaspoons vanilla extract
2 cups all-purpose flour
¾ cup HERSHEY'S Cocoa
1 teaspoon baking soda
½ teaspoon salt
2 cups (12-ounce package)
    HERSHEY'S Semi-Sweet
    Chocolate Chips
1 cup chopped dried apricots
1 cup coarsely chopped macadamia
    nuts

1. Heat oven to 350°F. Beat butter and sugar in large bowl until light and fluffy. Add eggs and vanilla; beat well. Stir together flour, cocoa, baking soda and salt; blend into butter mixture. Stir in chocolate chips, apricots and nuts.

2. Using ice cream scoop or ¼ cup measuring cup, drop dough onto ungreased cookie sheet.

3. Bake 12 to 14 minutes or until set. Cool slightly; remove from cookie sheet to wire rack. Cool completely.

*Makes about 2 dozen
(3½ inch) cookies*

Fruitcake Slices

1 cup butter or margarine, softened
1 cup powdered sugar
1 egg
1 teaspoon vanilla extract
1½ cups coarsely chopped candied fruit (fruitcake mix)
½ cup coarsely chopped walnuts
2½ cups all-purpose unsifted flour, divided
¾ to 1 cup flaked coconut

Beat butter in large bowl with electric mixer at medium speed until smooth. Add powdered sugar; beat until well blended. Add egg and vanilla; beat until well blended.

Combine candied fruit and walnuts in medium bowl. Stir ¼ cup flour into fruit mixture. Add remaining 2¼ cups flour to butter mixture; beat at low speed until blended. Stir in fruit mixture with spoon.

Shape dough into 2 logs, each about 2 inches in diameter and 5½ inches long. Spread coconut evenly on sheet of waxed paper. Roll logs in coconut, coating evenly. Wrap each log in plastic wrap. Refrigerate 2 to 3 hours or overnight, or freeze up to 1 month. (Let frozen logs stand at room temperature about 10 minutes before slicing and baking.)

Preheat oven to 350°F. Grease cookie sheets. Cut logs into ¼-inch-thick slices; place 1 inch apart on cookie sheets.

Bake 13 to 15 minutes or until edges are golden brown. Transfer to wire racks to cool. *Makes about 4 dozen cookies*

Honey Ginger Snaps

2 cups all-purpose flour
1 tablespoon ground ginger
2 teaspoons baking soda
⅛ teaspoon salt
⅛ teaspoon ground cloves
½ cup vegetable shortening
¼ cup butter, softened
1½ cups sugar, divided
¼ cup honey
1 egg
1 teaspoon vanilla

Preheat oven to 350°F. Grease cookie sheets. Combine flour, ginger, baking soda, salt and cloves in medium bowl.

Beat shortening and butter in large bowl with electric mixer at medium speed until smooth. Gradually beat in 1 cup sugar until blended; increase speed to high and beat until light and fluffy. Beat in honey, egg and vanilla until fluffy. Gradually stir in flour mixture until blended.

Shape mixture into 1-inch balls. Place remaining ½ cup sugar in shallow bowl; roll balls in sugar to coat. Place 2 inches apart on prepared cookie sheets.

Bake 10 minutes or until golden brown. Let cookies stand on cookie sheets 5 minutes; transfer to wire racks to cool completely. *Makes 42 cookies*

Fruitcake Slices

Oatmeal Almond Balls

⅓ cup honey
2 egg whites
½ teaspoon ground cinnamon
⅛ teaspoon salt
1½ cups uncooked quick oats
¼ cup sliced almonds, toasted

1. Preheat oven to 350°F. Combine honey, egg whites, cinnamon and salt in large bowl; mix well. Add oats and toasted almonds; mix well.

2. Drop by rounded teaspoonfuls onto ungreased nonstick cooking sheet. Bake 12 minutes or until lightly browned. Remove to wire rack to cool.
Makes 24 servings

Thumbprint Cookies

1 cup butter or margarine
¼ cup sugar
1 teaspoon almond extract
2 cups all-purpose flour
½ teaspoon salt
1 cup finely chopped nuts, if desired
SMUCKER'S® Preserves or Jams (any flavor)

Combine butter and sugar; beat until light and fluffy. Blend in almond extract. Add flour and salt; mix well.

Shape level tablespoonfuls of dough into balls; roll in nuts. Place on ungreased cookie sheets; flatten slightly. Indent centers; fill with preserves or jams.

Bake at 400°F for 10 to 12 minutes or just until lightly browned.
Makes 2½ dozen cookies

Snow-Covered Almond Crescents

1 cup (2 sticks) margarine or butter, softened
¾ cup powdered sugar
½ teaspoon almond extract *or* 2 teaspoons vanilla extract
2 cups all-purpose flour
¼ teaspoon salt (optional)
1 cup QUAKER® Oats (quick or old-fashioned, uncooked)
½ cup finely chopped almonds
Additional powdered sugar

Preheat oven to 325°F. Beat margarine, ¾ cup powdered sugar and almond extract until fluffy. Add flour and salt; mix until well blended. Stir in oats and almonds. Shape level measuring tablespoonfuls of dough into crescents. Place on ungreased cookie sheet about 2 inches apart.

Bake 14 to 17 minutes or until bottoms are light golden brown. Remove to wire rack. Sift additional powdered sugar generously over warm cookies. Cool completely. Store tightly covered.
Makes about 4 dozen cookies

Oatmeal Almond Balls

Cookie Cutter Cutouts

Jolly Peanut Butter Gingerbread Cookies

1⅔ cups (10-ounce package) REESE'S® Peanut
    Butter Chips
¾ cup (1½ sticks) butter or margarine,
    softened
1 cup packed light brown sugar
1 cup dark corn syrup
2 eggs
5 cups all-purpose flour
1 teaspoon baking soda
½ teaspoon ground cinnamon
¼ teaspoon ground ginger
¼ teaspoon salt

continued on page 70

68

Jolly Peanut Butter Gingerbread Cookies, continued

1. Place peanut butter chips in small microwave-safe bowl. Microwave at HIGH (100%) 1 to 2 minutes or until chips are melted when stirred. Beat melted peanut butter chips and butter in large bowl until well blended. Add brown sugar, corn syrup and eggs; beat until light and fluffy. Stir together flour, baking soda, cinnamon, ginger and salt. Add half of flour mixture to butter mixture; beat on low speed of electric mixer until smooth. Stir in remaining flour mixture with wooden spoon until well blended. Divide into thirds; wrap each in plastic wrap. Refrigerate at least 1 hour or until dough is firm enough to roll.

2. Heat oven to 325°F.

3. Roll 1 dough portion at a time to ⅛-inch thickness on lightly floured surface. Cut into holiday shapes with floured cookie cutters. Place on ungreased cookie sheet.

4. Bake 10 to 12 minutes or until set and lightly browned. Cool slightly; remove from cookie sheet to wire rack. Cool completely. Frost and decorate as desired.

Makes about 6 dozen cookies

Holiday Bits Cutout Cookies

1 cup (2 sticks) butter or margarine, softened
1 cup sugar
2 eggs
2 teaspoons vanilla extract
2½ cups all-purpose flour
½ teaspoon baking powder
½ teaspoon salt
HERSHEY'S Holiday Candy Coated Bits

1. Beat butter, sugar, eggs and vanilla in large bowl on low speed of electric mixer just until blended. Stir together flour, baking powder and salt; add to butter mixture, stirring until well blended.

2. Divide dough in half. Cover; refrigerate 1 to 2 hours or until firm enough to handle. Heat oven to 400°F. On lightly floured surface, roll each half of the dough to about ¼ inch thick.

3. Cut into tree, wreath, star or other shapes with 2½-inch cookie cutters. Place on ungreased cookie sheet. Press candy coated bits into cutouts.

4. Bake 6 to 8 minutes or until edges are firm and bottoms are very lightly browned. Remove from cookie sheet to wire rack. Cool completely.

Makes about 3½ dozen cookies

Holiday Bits Cutout Cookies

Christmas Cookie Pops

1 package (20 ounces) refrigerated
sugar cookie dough
All-purpose flour (optional)
20 to 24 (4-inch) lollipop sticks
Royal Icing (recipe follows)
6 ounces almond bark (vanilla or
chocolate), or butterscotch
chips
Vegetable shortening
Assorted small candies

1. Preheat oven to 350°F. Grease cookie sheets; set aside.

2. Remove dough from wrapper according to package directions.

3. Sprinkle dough with flour to minimize sticking, if necessary. Cut dough in half. Reserve 1 half; refrigerate remaining dough.

4. Roll reserved dough to ⅓-inch thickness. Cut out cookies using 3¼- or 3½-inch Christmas cookie cutters. Place lollipop sticks on cookies so that tips of sticks are imbedded in cookies. Carefully turn cookies with spatula so sticks are in back; place on prepared cookie sheets. Repeat with remaining dough.

5. Bake 7 to 11 minutes or until edges are lightly browned. Cool cookies on sheets 2 minutes. Remove cookies to wire racks; cool completely.

6. Prepare Royal Icing.

7. Melt almond bark in medium microwavable bowl according to package directions. Add 1 or more tablespoons shortening if coating is too thick. Hold cookies over bowl; spoon coating over cookies. Scrape excess coating from cookie edges. Decorate with Royal Icing and small candies immediately. Place cookies on wire racks set over waxed paper; let dry.

Makes 20 to 24 cookies

Royal Icing

2 to 3 egg whites
2 to 4 cups powdered sugar
1 tablespoon lemon juice
Liquid food coloring (optional)

Beat 2 egg whites in medium bowl with electric mixer until peaks just begin to hold their shape. Add 2 cups sugar and lemon juice; beat for 1 minute. If consistency is too thin for piping, gradually add more sugar until desired result is achieved; if it is too thick, add another egg white. Divide icing among several small bowls and tint to desired colors. Keep bowls tightly covered until ready to use.

Christmas Cookie Pops

Holiday Chocolate Shortbread Cookies

1 cup (2 sticks) butter, softened
1¼ cups powdered sugar
1 teaspoon vanilla extract
½ cup HERSHEY₌S Dutch
    Processed Cocoa or
    HERSHEY₌S Cocoa
1¾ cups all-purpose flour
1⅔ cups (10-ounce package)
    HERSHEY₌S Premier White
    Chips

1. Heat oven to 300°F. Beat butter, powdered sugar and vanilla in large bowl until creamy. Add cocoa; beat until well blended. Gradually add flour; stir well.

2. Roll or pat dough to ¼-inch thickness on lightly floured surface or between 2 pieces of wax paper. Cut into holiday shapes using star, tree, wreath or other cookie cutters. Reroll dough scraps, cutting cookies until dough is used. Place on ungreased cookie sheet.

3. Bake 15 to 20 minutes or just until firm. Immediately place white chips, flat side down, in decorative design on warm cookies. Cool slightly; remove from cookie sheet to wire rack. Cool completely.
*Makes about 4½ dozen
(2-inch diameter) cookies*

Note: For more even baking, place similar shapes and sizes of cookies on same cookie sheet.

Prep Time: 30 minutes

Bake Time: 15 minutes

Cool Time: 30 minutes

Chocolate Reindeer

1 cup butter or margarine, softened
1 cup sugar
1 egg
1 teaspoon vanilla
2 ounces semisweet chocolate,
    melted
2¼ cups all-purpose flour
1 teaspoon baking powder
¼ teaspoon salt
    Royal Icing (recipe follows)
    Assorted small candies

1. Beat butter and sugar in large bowl at high speed of electric mixer until fluffy. Beat in egg and vanilla. Add melted chocolate; mix well. Add flour, baking powder and salt; mix well. Cover and refrigerate about 2 hours or until firm.

2. Preheat oven to 325°F. Grease 2 cookie sheets; set aside.

3. Divide dough in half. Reserve 1 half; wrap remaining dough in plastic wrap and refrigerate.

4. Roll reserved dough on well-floured surface to ¼-inch thickness. Cut with reindeer cookie cutter. Place 2 inches apart on prepared cookie sheet. Chill 10 minutes.

5. Bake 13 to 15 minutes or until set. Cool completely on cookie sheets. Repeat steps with remaining dough.

6. Prepare Royal Icing. To decorate, pipe assorted colored icing on reindeer and add small candies.
Makes 16 (4-inch) reindeer

Royal Icing

2 to 3 egg whites
2 to 4 cups powdered sugar
1 tablespoon lemon juice
   Liquid food coloring (optional)

Beat 2 egg whites in medium bowl with electric mixer until peaks just begin to hold their shape. Add 2 cups sugar and lemon juice; beat 1 minute. If consistency is too thin for piping, gradually add more sugar until desired result is achieved; if it is too thick, add another egg white. Divide icing among several small bowls and tint to desired colors. Keep bowls tightly covered until ready to use.

Note: For best results, let cookies dry overnight, uncovered, before storing in airtight container at room temperature.

Gingerbread Cookies

   ¾ cup light or dark molasses
   ¾ cup FLEISCHMANN'S® Original
      Margarine
   ¾ cup packed light brown sugar
  4½ cups all-purpose flour
   1 tablespoon ground ginger
   2 teaspoons ground cinnamon
   1 teaspoon DAVIS® Baking Powder
   ½ teaspoon baking soda
   ½ teaspoon ground nutmeg
   ¼ cup EGG BEATERS® Healthy Real
      Egg Substitute
   Decorator icing, raisins and
      assorted candies, optional

1. Heat molasses, margarine and brown sugar in saucepan over medium heat to a boil, stirring occasionally. Remove from heat; cool.

2. Mix flour, ginger, cinnamon, baking powder, baking soda and nutmeg in large bowl. Blend egg substitute into molasses mixture. Stir molasses mixture into flour mixture until smooth. Wrap dough; refrigerate 1 hour.

3. Divide dough in half. Roll dough to ¼-inch thickness on floured surface. Cut with floured 5×3-inch gingerbread man cutter. Place onto lightly greased baking sheets.

4. Bake in preheated 350°F oven for 10 to 12 minutes or until lightly browned. Remove from sheets; cool on wire racks. Decorate as desired with icing, raisins and candies.   *Makes 2 dozen cookies*

Preparation Time: 30 minutes
Chill Time: 1 hour
Cook Time: 10 minutes
Total Time: 1 hour and 40 minutes

Christmas Tree Platter

Christmas Ornament Cookie Dough (recipe follows)
2 cups sifted powdered sugar
2 tablespoons milk or lemon juice
Assorted food colors, colored sugars and assorted small decors

1. Prepare Christmas Ornament Cookie Dough. Divide dough in half. Reserve 1 half; refrigerate remaining dough. Roll reserved half of dough to ⅛-inch thickness.

2. Preheat oven to 350°F. Cut out tree shapes with cookie cutters. Place on ungreased cookie sheets.

3. Bake 10 to 12 minutes or until edges are lightly browned. Remove to wire racks; cool completely.

4. Repeat with remaining half of dough. Reroll scraps; cut into small circles for ornaments, squares and rectangles for gift boxes and tree trunks.

5. Bake 8 to 12 minutes, depending on size of cookies.

6. Mix powdered sugar and milk for icing. Tint most of icing green and a smaller amount red or other colors for ornaments and boxes. Spread green icing on trees. Sprinkle ornaments and boxes with colored sugars or decorate as desired.

7. Arrange cookies on flat platter to resemble tree as shown in photo.
Makes about 1 dozen cookies

Christmas Ornament Cookie Dough

2¼ cups all-purpose flour
¼ teaspoon salt
1 cup granulated sugar
¾ cup butter or margarine, softened
1 egg
1 teaspoon vanilla
1 teaspoon almond extract

Combine flour and salt in medium bowl. Beat sugar and butter in large bowl at medium speed of electric mixer until fluffy. Beat in egg, vanilla and almond extract. Gradually add flour mixture. Beat at low speed until well blended. Form dough into 2 discs; wrap in plastic wrap and refrigerate 30 minutes or until firm.

Helpful Hint

Use this beautiful Christmas Tree Platter cookie as your centerpiece for this holiday's family dinner. It is sure to receive lots of "oohs" and "ahs!"

Stained Glass Cookies

½ cup FLEISCHMANN'S® Original Margarine, softened
½ cup sugar
½ cup honey
¼ cup EGG BEATERS® Healthy Real Egg Substitute
1 teaspoon vanilla extract
3 cups all-purpose flour
1 teaspoon DAVIS® Baking Powder
½ teaspoon baking soda
½ teaspoon salt
5 (.90-ounce) rolls Five Flavor or Fancy Fruits LIFE SAVERS® Candy

1. Beat together margarine, sugar, honey, egg substitute and vanilla in bowl with mixer until creamy. Mix in flour, baking powder, baking soda and salt. Cover; refrigerate at least 2 hours.

2. Roll dough on a lightly floured surface to ¼-inch thickness. Cut dough into desired shapes with 2½- to 3-inch floured cookie cutters. Trace a smaller version of cookie shape on dough leaving a ½- to ¾-inch border of dough. Cut out and remove dough from center of cookies; set aside. Place cut-out shapes on baking sheets lined with foil. Repeat with reserved dough, re-rolling scraps as necessary.

3. Crush each color of candy separately between two layers of wax paper. Spoon crushed candy inside centers of cut-out cookie shapes.

4. Bake in preheated 350°F oven for 6 to 8 minutes or until candy is melted and cookies are lightly browned. Cool cookies completely before removing from foil.

Makes 3½ dozen

Preparation Time: 1 hour
Chill Time: 2 hours
Cook Time: 6 minutes
Total Time: 3 hours and 6 minutes

Butter Cookies

¾ cup butter or margarine, softened
¼ cup granulated sugar
¼ cup packed light brown sugar
1 egg yolk
1¾ cups all-purpose flour
¾ teaspoon baking powder
⅛ teaspoon salt

1. Combine butter, sugars and egg yolk in medium bowl. Add flour, baking powder and salt; mix well. Cover; refrigerate until firm, about 4 hours or overnight.

2. Preheat oven to 350°F.

3. Roll dough on lightly floured surface to ¼-inch thickness; cut into desired shapes with cookie cutters. Place on ungreased cookie sheets.

4. Bake 8 to 10 minutes or until edges begin to brown. Remove to wire racks; cool completely.

Makes about 2 dozen cookies

Stained Glass Cookies

Extra-Special Cookies

Molded Scotch Shortbread

1½ cups all-purpose flour
¼ teaspoon salt
¾ cup butter, softened
⅓ cup sugar
1 egg

Preheat oven to temperature recommended by shortbread mold manufacturer. Combine flour and salt in medium bowl. Beat butter and sugar in large bowl with electric mixer at medium speed until light and fluffy. Beat in egg. Gradually add flour mixture; beat at low speed. Spray 10-inch ceramic shortbread mold with nonstick cooking spray. Press dough firmly into mold. Bake, cool and remove from mold according to manufacturer's directions.

Makes 1 shortbread mold

Almond Crescents

1 cup butter, softened
⅓ cup granulated sugar
1¾ cups all-purpose flour
¼ cup cornstarch
1 teaspoon vanilla
1½ cups ground toasted almonds*
Chocolate Glaze (recipe follows)
and powdered sugar

*To toast almonds, spread on cookie sheet. Bake at 325°F for 4 minutes or until fragrant and golden.

Preheat oven to 325°F. Beat butter and granulated sugar in large bowl until creamy. Mix in flour, cornstarch and vanilla. Stir in almonds. Shape tablespoonfuls of dough into crescents. Place 2 inches apart on ungreased cookie sheets. Bake 22 to 25 minutes or until light brown. Cool 1 minute. Remove to wire racks; cool completely. Prepare Chocolate Glaze; drizzle over cookies. Allow chocolate to set. Before serving, sprinkle with powdered sugar.

Makes about 3 dozen cookies

Chocolate Glaze: Place ½ cup semisweet chocolate chips and 1 tablespoon butter or margarine in small resealable plastic food storage bag. Place bag in bowl of hot water for 2 to 3 minutes or until chocolate is softened. Dry with paper towel. Knead until chocolate mixture is smooth. Cut off very tiny corner of bag. Drizzle chocolate mixture over cookies.

Chocolate Covered Cherry Cookies

1 cup sugar
½ cup butter, softened
1 egg
1½ teaspoons vanilla
1½ cups all-purpose flour
¼ cup unsweetened cocoa powder
¼ teaspoon baking powder
¼ teaspoon baking soda
¼ teaspoon salt
42 maraschino cherries, drained
reserving 4 to 5 teaspoons juice
1 (6-ounce) package semisweet chocolate pieces
½ cup sweetened condensed milk

Beat sugar and butter in large bowl until light and fluffy. Blend in egg and vanilla. Combine flour, cocoa, baking powder, baking soda and salt in small bowl. Add to sugar mixture; mix well. Shape dough into 1-inch balls; place on ungreased cookie sheet. Indent centers; fill each with 1 cherry. Combine chocolate pieces and sweetened condensed milk in small saucepan; stir over low heat until smooth. Blend in enough cherry juice to reach spreading consistency. Drop 1 teaspoon chocolate mixture over each cherry, spreading to cover cherry. Bake in preheated 350°F oven 12 minutes or until set.

Makes 3½ dozen cookies

Favorite recipe from **Wisconsin Milk Marketing Board**

Almond Crescents

Danish Cookie Rings

½ cup blanched almonds
2 cups all-purpose flour
¾ cup sugar
¼ teaspoon baking powder
1 cup butter, cut into small pieces
1 egg
1 tablespoon milk
1 tablespoon vanilla
8 candied red cherries
16 candied green cherries

Grease cookie sheets; set aside. Process almonds in food processor until ground, but not pasty. Place almonds, flour, sugar and baking powder in large bowl. Cut butter into flour mixture with pastry blender or 2 knives until mixture is crumbly.

Beat egg, milk and vanilla in small bowl with fork until well blended. Add egg mixture to flour mixture; stir until soft dough forms.

Spoon dough into pastry bag fitted with medium star tip. Pipe 3-inch rings 2 inches apart onto prepared cookie sheets. Refrigerate rings 15 minutes or until firm.

Preheat oven to 375°F. Cut cherries into halves. Cut each red cherry half into quarters; cut each green cherry half into 4 slivers. Press red cherry quarter onto each ring where ends meet. Arrange 2 green cherry slivers on either side of red cherry to form leaves. Bake 8 to 10 minutes or until golden. Remove cookies to wire racks; cool completely.

Makes about 5 dozen cookies

Mocha Biscotti

2½ cups all-purpose flour
½ cup unsweetened cocoa
2 teaspoons DAVIS® Baking Powder
1¼ cups sugar
¾ cup egg substitute
¼ cup margarine or butter, melted
4 teaspoons instant coffee powder
½ teaspoon vanilla extract
⅓ cup PLANTERS® Slivered
Almonds, chopped
Powdered sugar (optional)

1. Mix flour, cocoa and baking powder in small bowl; set aside.

2. Beat sugar, egg substitute, melted margarine, coffee powder and vanilla in large bowl with mixer at medium speed for 2 minutes. Stir in flour mixture and almonds.

3. Divide dough in half. Shape each portion of dough with floured hands into 14×2-inch log on greased baking sheet. (Dough will be sticky). Bake in preheated 350°F oven for 25 minutes.

4. Remove from oven and cut each log on a diagonal into 16 (1-inch) slices. Place biscotti, cut-side up, on baking sheets; return to oven and bake 10 to 15 minutes more on each side or until lightly toasted.

5. Remove from sheets. Cool completely on wire racks. Dust biscotti tops with powdered sugar if desired. Store in airtight container. *Makes 32 biscotti*

Preparation Time: 20 minutes

Cook Time: 35 minutes

Total Time: 55 minutes

Danish Cookie Rings

Linzer Sandwich Cookies

1⅓ cups all-purpose flour
¼ teaspoon baking powder
¼ teaspoon salt
¾ cup granulated sugar
½ cup butter, softened
1 egg
1 teaspoon vanilla
Powdered sugar (optional)
Seedless raspberry jam

Combine flour, baking powder and salt in small bowl. Beat granulated sugar and butter in medium bowl with electric mixer at medium speed until light and fluffy. Beat in egg and vanilla. Gradually add flour mixture. Beat at low speed until dough forms. Divide dough in half; cover and refrigerate 2 hours or until firm.

Preheat oven to 375°F. Working with 1 portion at a time, roll out dough on lightly floured surface to ³⁄₁₆-inch thickness. Cut dough into desired shapes with floured cookie cutters. Cut out equal numbers of each shape. (If dough becomes too soft, refrigerate several minutes before continuing.) Cut 1-inch centers out of half the cookies of each shape. Reroll trimmings and cut out more cookies. Place cookies 1½ to 2 inches apart on ungreased cookie sheets. Bake 7 to 9 minutes or until edges are lightly brown. Let cookies stand on cookie sheets 1 to 2 minutes. Remove cookies to wire racks; cool completely.

Sprinkle cookies with holes with powdered sugar, if desired. Spread 1 teaspoon jam on flat side of whole cookies, spreading almost to edges. Place cookies with holes, flat side down, over jam to create sandwich.

Makes about 2 dozen cookies

Chunky Butter Christmas Cookies

1¼ cups butter, softened
1 cup packed brown sugar
½ cup dairy sour cream
1 egg
2 teaspoons vanilla
1½ cups all-purpose flour
1 teaspoon baking soda
1 teaspoon salt
1½ cups old fashioned or quick oats, uncooked
1 (10-ounce) package white chocolate pieces
1 cup flaked coconut
1 (3½-ounce) jar macadamia nuts, coarsely chopped

Beat butter and sugar in large bowl until light and fluffy. Blend in sour cream, egg and vanilla. Add combined flour, baking soda and salt; mix well. Stir in oats, white chocolate pieces, coconut and nuts. Drop rounded teaspoonfuls of dough, 2 inches apart, onto ungreased cookie sheet. Bake in preheated 375°F oven 10 to 12 minutes or until edges are lightly browned. Cool 1 minute; remove to cooling rack.

Makes 5 dozen cookies

Favorite recipe from **Wisconsin Milk Marketing Board**

Linzer Sandwich Cookies

Mincemeat Pastries

3½ **cups all-purpose flour**
 ¾ **cup granulated sugar**
 ½ **teaspoon salt**
 ½ **cup (1 stick) butter, chilled**
 8 **tablespoons vegetable shortening**
 1 **cup buttermilk**
 1 **cup mincemeat**
 ¼ **cup powdered sugar (optional)**

1. Combine flour, granulated sugar and salt in large bowl; set aside.

2. Cut butter into 1-inch chunks. Add butter and shortening to flour mixture. Cut in with pastry blender or 2 knives until mixture resembles coarse crumbs. Drizzle buttermilk over top; toss just until mixture comes together into a ball.

3. Turn out dough onto lightly floured work surface; fold in half and flatten to about ½ inch thick. Knead about eight times. Divide dough in half; press each half into ½-inch-thick disk. Wrap in plastic wrap and refrigerate at least 30 minutes.

4. Let dough rest at room temperature 10 minutes. Preheat oven to 350°F. Lightly grease cookie sheets; set aside. Roll one disk of dough into 18×12-inch rectangle on lightly floured work surface. Cut into 24 (3-inch) squares. Place heaping ½ teaspoon mincemeat in center of each square. Fold one corner about ⅔ of the way over the filling; fold opposite corner ⅔ of the way over the filling.

5. Place 2 inches apart on prepared cookie sheets. Repeat with remaining dough.

6. Bake 20 minutes or until lightly browned. Remove cookies to wire rack; cool completely. Sprinkle tops of pastries lightly with powdered sugar, if desired.
Makes 4 dozen cookies

Banana Crescents

½ **cup DOLE® Chopped Almonds, toasted**
 6 **tablespoons sugar, divided**
 ½ **cup margarine, cut into pieces**
1½ **cups plus 2 tablespoons all-purpose flour**
 ⅛ **teaspoon salt**
 1 **extra-ripe, medium DOLE® Banana, peeled**
 2 **to 3 ounces semisweet chocolate chips**

• Pulverize almonds with 2 tablespoons sugar.

• Beat margarine, almonds, remaining 4 tablespoons sugar, flour and salt.

• Purée banana; add to almond mixture and mix until well blended.

• Roll tablespoonfuls of dough into logs, then shape into crescents. Place on ungreased cookie sheet. Bake in 375°F oven 25 minutes or until golden. Cool on wire rack.

• Melt chocolate in microwavable dish at MEDIUM (50% power) 1½ to 2 minutes, stirring once. Dip ends of cookies in chocolate. Refrigerate until chocolate is set.
Makes 2 dozen cookies

Mincemeat Pastries

Date Pinwheel Cookies

1¼ cups dates, pitted and finely
   chopped
¾ cup orange juice
½ cup granulated sugar
1 tablespoon butter
3 cups plus 1 tablespoon
   all-purpose flour, divided
2 teaspoons vanilla, divided
4 ounces cream cheese
¼ cup vegetable shortening
1 cup packed brown sugar
2 eggs
1 teaspoon baking soda
½ teaspoon salt

1. Heat dates, orange juice, granulated sugar, butter and 1 tablespoon flour in medium saucepan over medium heat. Cook, stirring frequently, 10 minutes or until thick; remove from heat. Stir in 1 teaspoon vanilla; set aside to cool.

2. Beat cream cheese, shortening and brown sugar about 3 minutes in large bowl until light and fluffy. Add eggs and remaining 1 teaspoon vanilla; beat 2 minutes longer.

3. Combine 3 cups flour, baking soda and salt in medium bowl. Add to shortening mixture; stir just until blended. Divide dough in half. Roll one half of dough on lightly floured work surface into 12 × 9-inch rectangle. Spread half of date mixture over dough. Spread evenly, leaving ¼-inch border on top short edge. Starting at short side, tightly roll up dough jelly-roll style. Wrap in plastic wrap; freeze for at least 1 hour. Repeat with remaining dough.

4. Preheat oven to 350°F. Grease cookie sheets. Unwrap dough. Using heavy thread or dental floss, cut dough into ¼-inch slices. Place slices 1 inch apart on prepared cookie sheets.

5. Bake 12 minutes or until lightly browned. Let cookies stand on cookie sheets 2 minutes. Remove cookies to wire rack; cool completely.
Makes 6 dozen cookies

Make Ahead Tip

Wrap rolls of dough in plastic wrap and twist the ends tightly to seal. Place wrapped rolls in tall plastic drinking glasses before freezing so rolls will not flatten from resting on freezer shelf.

Date Pinwheel Cookies

Acknowledgments

The publisher would like to thank the following companies and organizations listed below for the use of their recipes and photographs in this publication.

Blue Diamond Growers®

Dole Food Company, Inc.

Duncan Hines® brand is a registered trademark of Aurora Foods Inc.

Fleischmann's® Original Spread

Hershey Foods Corporation

Hunt-Wesson, Inc.

Kahlúa® Liqueur

Kraft Foods, Inc.

M&M/MARS

OREO® Cookies

The Procter & Gamble Company

The Quaker® Kitchens

The J.M. Smucker Company

Wisconsin Milk Marketing Board

Index